U.S. 7th Cavalry Patrol, 1880

Poilu, by Marcel Baldet
1916

Champlain,
1609

French Chasseur
à Cheval de la Gard
1810

ACKNOWLEDGEMENTS

We wish to express our grateful appreciation to Mr. Marcel Baldet, Secretary-General of Le Sabretache and Mr. Eugene Leliepvre, Peintre de l'Armee, for their assistance with European collections, and to Messrs. William Imrie, Richard Riehn, Clyde Risley, and Andrew Zaremba for valued technical and historical advice.

Our thankful appreciation also goes to the collectors who so kindly permitted us to photograph their military miniatures: Mr. Donald Burgess pp 6*, 19*; Mr. Peter Dattilo pp 34, 35; Miss Josaine Desfontaines pp 8, 36; Mr. Fernand Gravet p 43a; Mr. William Imrie–Mr. Clyde Risley pp 22, 23, 37, 40, 41; Mr. Eugene Leliepvre pp 42, 43b; Lexington Historical Society p 18c; Mr. James Linen pp 25, 26, 27; Mr. Joseph McGerr pp 11*, 17*; Mr. Richard Riehn pp 9, 14, 16, 39a*b; Mr. Lucien Rousselot pp 44, 45; Mr. Arnold Sherman pp 12, 13; Mr. Alan Silk p 38b*; Mr. Philip Stearns pp 7, 24, 32*, 33*; West Point Museum p 10; author's collection pp 18a–b, 19, 20, 21, 28, 29, 30, 31, 38a–c–d. (* painted by the collector)

Military miniatures professionally created by R. Courtenay, London, pp 12, 13; J. Desfontaines, Paris, pp 7, 8, 18, 19, 24, 28a, 36, 37a–b; Russel Gammage, London, p 6; John Greenwood, London, p 10; Imrie-Risley Miniatures, Richmond Hill, N.Y., pp 20 through 23, 37c, 40, 41; Jack Scheid, Easton, Pa., p 18c; W. Scholtz-Bunzel, Berlin, pp 14, 16; Charles Stadden (Norman Newton, Ltd.), London, pp 6, 11, 15, 17, 25 through 28b–c, 29 through 35, 38a–d, 39a–b.

MILITARY MINIATURES

BY PETER BLUM

PHOTOGRAPHS BY PHILLIP STEARNS

THE ODYSSEY PRESS · NEW YORK

MILITARY MINIATURES, themselves a reflection of history, go far back in the past, at least as far as the Egyptians, who placed carved wooden soldiers in the tombs of the dead. And military miniatures have played a part in the lives of a number of historical personages. As a child, Louis XIV of France had an army of silver soldiers, which were passed on to the Dauphin. Napoleon used figurines to plan his coronation as emperor. ■ But military miniatures were not

LEFT: *The Egyptian Pharoah Thut-Mose III, leading his chariot division in pursuit of the Syrians. The figures are 2¼ inches tall.* RIGHT: *Egyptian warriors mounted on a mighty war elephant. Unlike most miniatures, this was not cast from a mold, but sculpted directly in metal by Mlle. Josainne Desfontaine.*

ABOVE: *Occasionally, makers of military miniatures take their subjects from court life. Here a medieval lord and lady are hunting with falcons, a favorite sport of the period. The figures of the man and woman are 2¼ inches tall.* OPPOSITE PAGE: *The 14th-century knight carrying the standard of Burgundy is a "flat," 1¼ inch tall. The figures in the background are unpainted flats.*

produced in any quantity until the early 1800's, when German workshops began turning out "flats"—one-dimensional figures—cast in tin, and then in a more durable alloy of tin and lead. Production of fully rounded three-dimensional figures began in the 1900's, and the art has reached its height only during the last fifteen years. At first considered mere toy soldiers for children, the miniatures soon attracted the attention of adults. Today they are avidly collected by thousands of persons, and are exhibited, often in dioramas, in military museums. ∎
It is easy to understand the fascination of these small figures. The result of painstaking research and meticulous craftsmanship, they are history that can be held in the palm of the hand. To a collector, historical accuracy is even more important than artistry. An inaccurate figure, no matter how colorful, has little value; an accurate figure, with every detail of costume true to

its period, is a re-creation of the past. ■ The first step in the making of military miniatures is always research. Then, a sculptor fashions a master figure, in either clay or metal, and from this a mold is made. The miniatures are cast from the mold in much the same manner as fine jewelry. Some miniatures are cast in one piece and then bent into the desired position; others are cast in several parts and then assembled in a variety of positions. Some French makers even dress the basic figure in uniforms cut from thin sheets of metal. Usually, fittings such as weapons and shields are cast separately and cemented or soldered to the figures. The last step is painting, and again research is necessary to ensure accuracy. Flat paint is used to represent cloth and glossy paint to represent leather or metal. Many collectors purchase unpainted castings and do their own painting, finding it a most satisfying aspect of their absorbing

hobby. The accuracy and skill with which the most minute details are painted determines the worth of the completed figure. Several hundred figures are generally cast from the same mold; it is the painting that makes the difference. ■ Military miniatures are made in many sizes, from 1 to more than 6 inches tall, but the most widely collected are the 2¼-inch, fully rounded figures. Unpainted, they range in price from $1.25 to $3.00 for a figure on foot, $6.00 to $25.00 for a mounted figure. Painted figures sell from $10.00 to as high as $200.00, and rarities of unusual size fetch even more. In this book, the miniatures are all recent productions. ■

LEFT: *This diorama of the Battle of Crecy in 1346 was especially created for the West Point Museum, using figures 1¼ inches tall. The battle marks an important point in the evolution of military tactics—it was the first time that foot soldiers vanquished the medieval mounted knight. The feat was accomplished by the English longbowmen.*

Small figure below is Robert Bruce, wearing the crown of Scotland, about 1300.

Henry V of England.

At Poitiers, in 1356, English and French knights met in fierce combat after the English longbowmen had taken a heavy toll of the enemy. The miniatures on these pages represent the climax of the battle, when the French knights fell back to defend their standard. Although a suit of 14th-century armor often weighed more than 60 pounds, it was so well articulated that the knights could move and wield their weapons

with ease. ■ In creating these 2¼-inch-tall knights, Richard Courtenay placed them in a variety of lifelike positions. The knights were distinguished from each other by the heraldic coat of arms painted on their shields and embroidered on the cloth surcoat worn over their armor. The coats of arms on the miniatures are historically accurate, the result of many hours of careful research and painstaking artistry.

Frederick the Great's battalions were faltering in the battle against the Russians at Zorndorf in 1758. Dismounting, Frederick seized the colors of the colonel of the Fusilier Regiment von Bulow and led the men forward himself. The two figures at the left that illustrate this moment in history are flats only slightly more than 1¼-inch tall; skillful painting has made them look three-dimensional. ■ The fully round miniatures at the right represent a group of Frederick's Prussian cavalry officers in parade dress uniforms. The officer with the leopard skin over his shoulder is a Zieten hussar. The hussar officer on the far right wears his blue pelisse draped typically over the left shoulder. The white fur trim was made realistic by building up and texturing the paint. The three officers in white uniforms and breastplates are cuirassiers. The cuirass—a breastplate—protected both the breast and back of the wearer.

"I intend, in spite of the rules of war, to attack...." So said Frederick the Great to his officers just before the Battle of Leuthen on the snowy night of December 3, 1757. He meant to take the offensive, although his Prussian troops numbered only 35,000 to the Austrians' 65,000. It was the Seven Years' War, and Frederick faced a coalition that included Austria, France, Russia, and Sweden. ■ The figures are flats, each representing a particular officer known to have been on the scene. They are painted on both sides, so that their faces are visible on the side turned away from the camera. The trees are made of bare metal, and fine sugar has been used to give the effect of snow. This group of figures, like many of the others in this book, are being produced today and are available to collectors who want to do their own painting. ■ On the right is a portrait figure of Frederick late in his career. The painting of the face is noteworthy. The technique is much like that of stage make-up. Light flesh tones accentuate the nose and chin; darker tones around the eyes and cheeks give the impression of age and fatigue. All this has been accomplished in an area no larger than that of a pea.

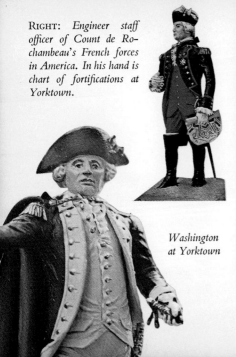

RIGHT: *Engineer staff officer of Count de Rochambeau's French forces in America. In his hand is chart of fortifications at Yorktown.*

Washington at Yorktown

ABOVE: *Lexington, just before "the shot heard round the world" and the first battle of the American Revolution.* OPPOSITE PAGE: *A scene at Yorktown, the last battle of the Revolution.*

The diorama by John Scheid of the first battle of the American Revolution, on Lexington Common, is based on journals and diaries kept by eyewitnesses of the fighting. Each of the principal figures precisely represents a soldier involved in the action. The buildings in the diorama are facsimiles of the ones that stood on the old commons and are in perfect scale to the figures. Major Pitcairn of the Royal Marines, mounted on his horse, is shown ordering the Minute Men to disperse as his British regulars form ranks and prepare to fire the first shots of the war. The main force of redcoats—six companies—can be seen in the distance, marching up the road from Boston. ■ At the right are exceptionally fine portrait figures of General Washington and the Marquis de Lafayette looking over the fortifications at Yorktown. The uniforms of these figures, created in France by Mlle. Josaine Desfontaines, were made by draping the castings with thin metal sheeting cut to a pattern, much as a tailor cuts cloth for a suit. Cuffs and lapels are turned back, just as they were on the original uniforms. Even the buttons were made separately, as shown in the close-up of Washington at far left on page 18.

"No artillery better served than ours," wrote Washington after the Battle of Monmouth, in which the American artillery proved to be the equal of any in the world. These artillery scenes, especially created for this book by Imrie-Risley Miniatures of New York, faithfully follow in every detail plans in a *Treatise of Artillery* published in 1779. The wheels, gun

carriage, and limber were all cast in metal, then painted to resemble wood. ■ The guns were transported by civilian drivers and their teams. Often a farmer would contract to transport a field piece to a state line. Once there, he would set off for home, leaving the soldiers to get on as best they could. Later in the war, drivers were sometimes hired on a more regular basis.

During the Revolutionary War, the British 17th Light Dragoons, under the command of the infamous cavalry leader Colonel Banastre Tarleton, burst unexpectedly into the village of Poundridge, New York, where they surprised Colonel Elisha Sheldon's 2nd Continental Light Dragoons and chased them down the road toward Stamford, Connecticut. These scenes depict the moment when the redcoats overtook the Americans. In planning the diorama of this little-known skirmish, Imrie-Risley Miniatures studied contemporary news accounts and the official British Army report of the action. ■ Charles Smith, a specialist in miniature landscaping, designed the terrain. The rock fence is made of plaster, carved and painted to give the impression of stone. The grass is made of pieces of hemp string. No detail has been overlooked, from the horsehair crest on the brass dragoon helmet to the minute bit in the horse's mouth. ■ Philip Stearns photographed the diorama outdoors at what is now Pound Ridge, New York—the actual site of the battle. He used a special photographic technique to make the full-size trees in the distance blend perfectly with the diorama and the figures, which are 2¼ inches tall.

■ Napoleon Bonaparte, a favorite of both miniature designers and collectors, is shown here as he appeared during his successful Egyptian campaign. He was not yet Consul or Emperor, and he wears the uniform of a general. In the scabbard at his side is a scimitar, a Turkish-style weapon popular with military men at this time. His hat is typical of those worn by generals of the period. This figure, the only one of its kind, was created by Mlle. Desfontaines, who studies contemporary portraits of her subjects and accounts of their personal lives in order to understand their character. On page 25 are Napoleon and his staff at the start of the Russian campaign in 1812. The figures, by the noted English maker, Charles Stadden, are pictured against a contemporary map of Europe—the map Napoleon tried to change. ■ This group of miniatures, never before photographed, is one of the outstanding in the world.

Each of the figures is an accurate portrayal of a corps commander or officer of Napoleon's staff. Even the fact that Marshal Bessières still wore his hair in the long, old-fashioned style has not been overlooked. ■ UPPER LEFT, from left to right: General Roguet; General Fournier-Sarlovèze in uniform of 9th Hussars; cuirassier General Saint-Germain; General Colbert of the 2nd Lancers; Marshal Murat in hussar uniform; General Krasinski of 1st Polish Lancers (in the French service); a general of carabiniers. ■ LOWER LEFT: Marshal Berthier in uniform of chausseur *à Cheval de la Garde*; Napoleon, also in uniform of chausseur *à Cheval de la Garde*—his favorite; Colonel Baron Gourgaud, his aide; Marshal Bessières, Commander of the Imperial Guard Cavalry; Aide-de-Camp to the General Staff. ■ AT RIGHT: The same figures have been photographed outdoors and from a different angle to show the amazing detail.

Joachim Murat

Prince Eugene

General
Baron Colbert

*A grenadier
à Cheval de la Garde*

Joachim Murat, King of Naples, was one of Napoleon's greatest generals. Though the figure, including the horse, is just under 3½ inches tall, the gold lace stands out boldly against the red hussar uniform. The stirrups and straps were made separately and added to the figure. ■ Prince Eugene de Beauharnais was Napoleon's stepson and the son of Josephine. This figure shows how a miniature cast in one piece can be bent into an unusual position. ■ General Baron Colbert, the commander of the 2nd Lancers, served Napoleon loyally. His uniform is characteristic of the famous Polish lancers. The colorful headgear is a *czapka*. ■ The grenadier *à Cheval de la Garde* was one of the elite troops always in the vicinity of the Emperor. Details like the musket were cast separately and then added to the mounted figure. The sons of France's best families, to show their nobility, never wore the customary military mustache.

29

At left, the Duke of Wellington and members of his staff survey the terrain near Waterloo, Belgium, before the fateful battle that would crush Napoleon's hopes for world conquest. The "Iron Duke" peers through a telescope, while an aide, a light infantry officer, scans a map, and Lord Combermer, in the uniform of the 12th Light Dragoons, points out something of interest. Wellington is wearing an ordinary frock coat instead of a uniform coat—his usual practice in battle. He and Lord Combermer are carrying scimitars. Although the map is only slightly larger than a postage stamp, it accurately shows the topography of the battle area. ■ At right, Highlanders of the Black Watch, celebrating the British victory, have discarded their bonnets for French headgear. The Highlander at the left wears a marshal's hat and imitates Napoleon's hand-in-breast stance. The man on the right tries on an officer's pelisse.

Shown here are scenes from French camp life in the early nineteenth century. At left, a trumpeter of the French grenadiers *à Cheval* puts his horse through its paces as an officer looks on. To distinguish the trumpeter from the other soldiers of a regiment, he usually rode a white horse and wore a uniform of a different color. Also in contrasting uniforms are the dragoon officer and trumpeter in the background; on their heads are brass helmets with crests of horse hair. ■ AT UPPER RIGHT, a drum major introduces the drummer boy to a line officer and his lady. Drum majors are a favorite with collectors because of their elaborately decorated uniforms. Just how elaborate was the uniform of an actual drum major depended on the size of the regimental colonel's pocketbook; he had to pay for special uniforms out of his personal funds. ■ At LOWER RIGHT, the frolicsome young lady has commandeered the fur cap belonging to the Grenadier of the Imperial Guards, and is beating the drum with miniature drumsticks made of pins. The other soldier is a sapper, who marched at the head of a column to clear the way for the rest of the regiment. His beard, axe, and long leather apron are typical.

The stirring sound of military bands has changed little over the years. No longer in use, however, is the Jingling Johnny—bells on a colorful pole—here carried by the third figure from the left. ■ British regimental bands formally came into being with the Royal Warrant of 1768 as small units of eight musicians without percussion sections. When Turkish music became popular in the 1780's, elaborately dressed Negro musicians, playing tympanis and other percussion instruments, were added. ■ In line-regiment bands, the drummers and fifers were soldiers in the regular army. The other musicians were civilians hired by the regiment's colonel, who paid their salaries out of his own pocket. Bandsmen were subject to military authority, and as time passed they were drawn from the regular service. ■ According to legend, when General Cornwallis surrendered the British cause at Yorktown a British regi-

British Foot Guards Band of 1815. The drummers and fifers, who were regular army men, are wearing bearskin caps. The hired musicians wear shakos; the Negro musicians, also hired, wear turbans in the Turkish manner.

mental band played an appropriately named tune, "The World Turned Upside Down." ■ The bugle and the drum were the means of communication on the battlefields of yesterday's armies. The drums were decorated with the regimental coat of arms and battle honors, as were the banners of the kettle-drums carried by mounted units. Such drums were among the prize possessions of the regiment and were valiantly defended in battle. Because of their military significance and colorful trappings, figures of bandsmen, drummers, buglers, and pipers are highly popular with collectors. The miniature instruments are cast separately and then fitted into the hands of the musicians. ■ The Scottish Highland regiments have gone into battle to the skirl of bagpipes since 1678, when the Royal Scots first went into British service. The bagpiper on page 37, created by William Imrie, is a masterpiece of craftsmanship. Note how faithfully the Clan Gordon tartan has been reproduced.

A kettledrummer of the French carabiniers (cavalrymen armed with the short, light muskets known as carbines), of about 1800. The skill of the painter is shown in the accuracy of details, such as the $\frac{1}{4}$-inch-high gold eagle on the drum banner.

Drummer of the British Foot Guards, 1815

Drummer of the French Infantry, 1791

Gordon Highlander, about 1900

"The soldier is never in a foreign country when he is under the colors; where the colors are, there is France," said Napoleon's Council of State. And more than one regiment has died rather than suffer the shame of losing its colors in battle. ■ In miniatures, flags are made of thin sheet metal, draped to look like cloth and cemented or soldered to small metal rods used as staffs. The intricate details of the flag are painted on the folded surface. ■ The figures on page 38 are: (1) an infantryman of the French Revolutionary period carrying the colors of the 23rd Demi-Brigade and wearing wooden shoes, a patch on his knee, and a spoon in his hat; (2) an Austrian infantry officer of about 1812 with regimental colors; (3) a Black Watch Highlander with regimental colors; (4) an officer of the French Imperial Guard with regimental colors. The staff is topped by an eagle, personal symbol of Napoleon.

BELOW: *German* Garde du Corps *color bearer, about 1914.* RIGHT: *Officer of English Civil War period, with colors of the Holland Regiment.*

A dramatic incident from the first day of the great Battle of Gettysburg, the turning point of the Civil War, is depicted in the diorama at the left. Union General Buford's outnumbered cavalrymen are dismounting to fight a delaying action against the Confederates until the Union 1st Corps can come to their aid. The earth is painted plaster; the fence is of wood carved to resemble split rails and painted to look weather-beaten. ■ The diorama on the opposite page was specially designed by Imrie-Risley for this book. It captures the moment at Gettysburg when a courier reported to General Lee that the Confederates had made contact with the Union troops. Photographer Phillip Stearns photographed the figures outdoors against a background of real trees. The Confederate flag was printed on paper and then fixed to the staff. Everything is in perfect scale, including the binoculars held by one member of Lee's staff.

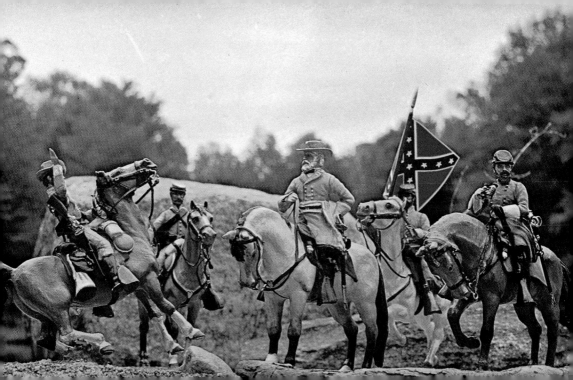

The first full regiment of French dragoons, formed by Louis XV in 1668, was not cavalry in the true sense of the word. These dragoons were mounted infantrymen who used their horses as transportation and then fought on foot. They took their name from the heavy muskets which they carried in addition to swords. In the latter part of the 18th century, when warfare became more complicated, there arose the need for light, mobile cavalry units to act as scouts and skirmishers. Hussar regiments, modeled after the Hungarian light cavalry, were formed. The hussars wore the most colorful and elaborate uniforms in Napoleon's Imperial Army. ■ The dragoon at left and the hussar at the far right are typical of their branches of the cavalry. Both figures are one of a kind and are of unusual size. They are 16 inches high and represent military miniature craftsmanship of the highest order. They were created by the noted French military historian, Eugene Leliepvre, an official artist for the French Army. The uniforms are made of cloth, stitched along the same seams as the full-size uniform, and the boots and gloves are of leather. The saddles and bridles are actually fastened by the tiny buckles.

ABOVE: *the two miniature French hussar uniforms are fashioned of cloth, and the shako-style headgear are made of leather. Only about 8 inches high, the uniform on the left depicts the 10th Hussars while the one at the right shows the 8th Hussars, ca. 1808. The miniature metal helmet at the left is a Genie, or engineer, headpiece.* RIGHT: *the Czapska is typical of the style worn by the Polish and Dutch lancers of Napoleon's Guard.*

In the mid-1600's, cavalry regiments were equipped with steel cuirasses, or breastplates. This holdover from medieval days served as good protection until the Franco-Prussian War of 1870, when modern firepower made body armor useless. Today such units as the British Household Cavalry still wear steel helmets and breastplates to perpetuate the splendor and pageantry of the past. ■ The mounted cuirassier of the 9th Regiment, at left, is a 16-inch-tall, dressed manikin. It was photographed in the miniature armory of its creator, the famed French military painter, Lucien Rousselot, another official artist of the French Army. The cuirasses and helmets were hammered out of steel, much in the manner of the originals. The sabers can be drawn from their scabbards and the tiny triggers operate the flint locks on the muskets. The uniforms, horse trappings, and weapons are all in perfect scale to the 16-inch cuirassier.

RIGHT: *The close-up shows the cuirassiers lifelike face and the remarkable detail of the helmet, including the regimental number 9 embossed on it.* BELOW: *A cuirassier painting and miniature equipment by Rousselot.*

Bengal Lancer, Indian Army

Napoleon and Grenadier

Roman General

Prussian Cavalry, 1750